How to Vote

Saskia Lacey

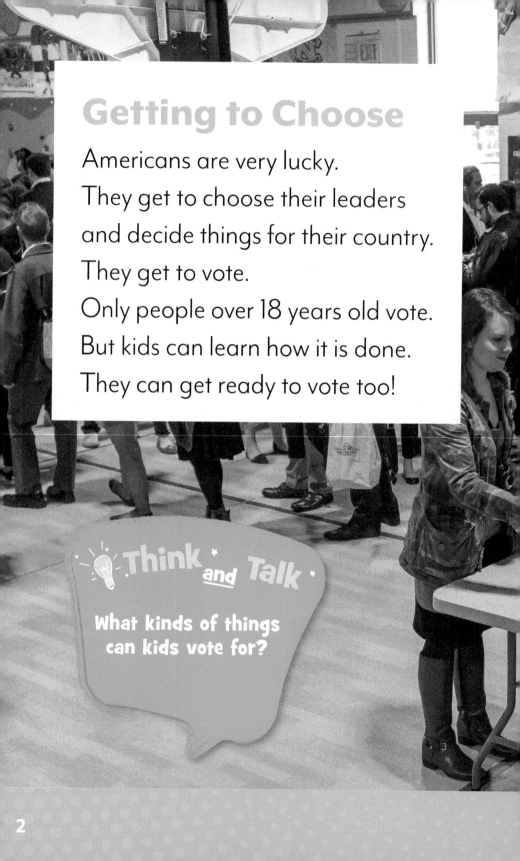

Getting to Choose

Americans are very lucky.
They get to choose their leaders
and decide things for their country.
They get to vote.
Only people over 18 years old vote.
But kids can learn how it is done.
They can get ready to vote too!

Think and Talk

What kinds of things can kids vote for?

At the Polls

Sam is happy to vote for his leaders.
He likes to have his voice heard.
Sam stands in line.
He waits his turn.

Sam goes inside the voting booth.
He reads the names.
Sam thinks hard.
Then, he makes his choice.

Back to Nonfiction

Before You Vote

Take time before you vote.
Learn as much as you can.

The Right to Vote

Voting is a right!
It is part of being a citizen.

Learn about who wants to lead.
Listen to what they say.
Think hard.

A Million Voices

Millions of people vote each year.
Each one has a voice.
Their vote is their voice.

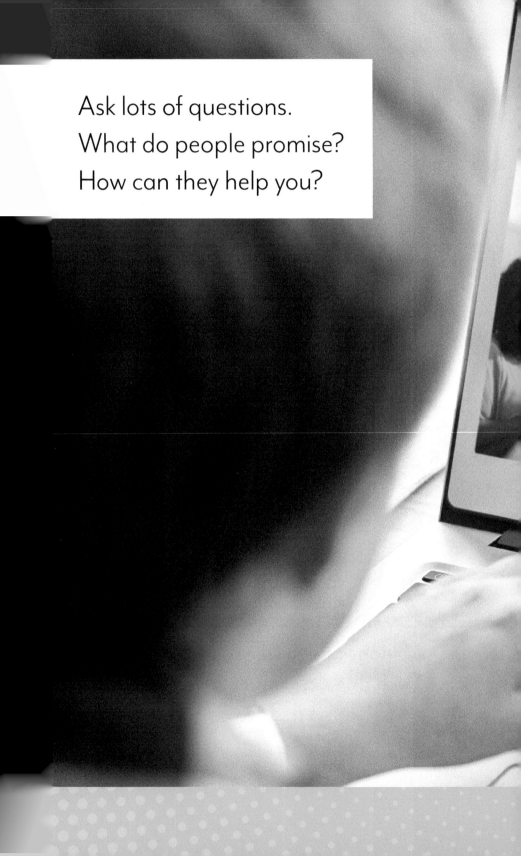

Ask lots of questions.
What do people promise?
How can they help you?

Think about each person.
What are their jobs?
What are their goals?
Who do you agree with?

Think and Talk

How can you tell what leaders want to do?

Now, it is time.

Who do you think should lead?

Choose the person you would vote for.

Free for All

You do not pay to vote.
Voting is free.

Ready, Set, Vote!

Now, you are ready.
It is time to cast your vote!

Your Eyes Only

Each person votes on their own. No one can see how you vote!

Go to the polls.

Cast your vote.

This is how Americans elect their leaders.

At the Polls

It can be busy at the polls.
Many people wait in line.
They take their turn.

Spread the Word

Tell your friends about voting.
Your vote is your voice!

Civics in Action

Grown-ups vote for America's leaders. But kids can vote for some things too.
Have an election with your family or friends.

1. Ask each voter to suggest a game to play. Write all the games in a list.

2. Give each voter a sheet of paper and a pencil.

3. Ask each voter to vote for their top choice. They should write one game on their paper.

4. Tally the votes. Which game has the most votes? Play it!